My Own Fires

poems by Harriett Van Os

ISBN-13: 978-0983421726
ISBN-10: 0983421722

First Printing, October 2011
Cover Design: Alyssa Morhardt-Goldstein

Brothel Books
The Poetry Society of New York
New York, New York
brothelbooks.com

CONTENTS

Interviews with Paul and Millicent Daily

Dark Body

To Theo

After

For Constantine

My Own Fires

Harriett Van Os walked here from Florida to be with you. You quiet the 17 ghosts that cling to her back, screaming. Take no notice of her peculiarities and let her spend a little time with you. She'll tell you secrets she doesn't know she knows.

Dream

I.

My crooked hands shake
something unreasonable.

I can see them
roasting on glowing coals.

I don't take them out.
I am always cold.
I am always letting off everything,

like a pan of water
on a stove
without a lid.

I escape almost silently.

Dream

II.

Babies! Babies everywhere and not
making any sounds.

I watched them crawl over
soft white blankets
their hands so small
their movements so sure.

When they almost collided
with one another, they'd sit
back on their diapers and stare.
They'd move their tiny hands
to their mouths. They'd suck awhile,
together, then roll over
and start crawling again
and again.

Mrs. Georgia Sands, former neighbor of Harriett Van Os
Interviewed by John Friedman in April 1963

Well, I lived in the neighborhood before they did. Back when it was called County Road, now it's Okeechobee. My husband built a little house for me, we were newlyweds, and we settled right in. Frank Van Os came from Miami and bought their house, about a quarter-mile down. It was brand-new, but the brothers who built it had a fallin' out and they all moved up to different parts of Tennessee, I think. Right after selling the house. And Frank was a newlywed too, this pretty girl Margot, I think she was barely eighteen but smart as a whip. And sweet! Anyhow, seeing as I'd been married near five years by then, I helped her get settled and we were fast friends. Harriett and Constantine were born about a year later.

She was a sweet baby, quiet, and not a lick of sickness or temper. And as she grew up, she was a great help to her mama. She basically raised all them kids that was younger than she. I think there were eighteen total— mind you, they did adopt Roger after the hurricane, and the triplets when their mama, Frank's sister-in-law, got sick. But that was a big bunch, the Van Os house.

Harriett wasn't too good at school, but she liked reading, so everybody passed her any books they had. I'm not sure when she ever got to them, she was so busy with the children, but she read them, quick as you can. And would tell you about them too, bless her heart; she could put you to sleep with all that talk! They pulled her out of school when her mama started working full-time at the dress shop, and she never really complained. I do think she was happier, she was about ten, then.

I don't recall her having any outside friends, but she was real close with her brother Constantine, and she had all the rest to keep her company. There was a boy, Hank Kelly, who took a real liking to her though, and word spread around that he was fixing to marry her. It was no great secret that she would have had him, I believe he put stars in her eyes the first day she ever saw him. And I was rooting for them, Hank was a good boy and Harriett would make a good wife. She was already a good mother.

But then the fire happened. They never figured out how it got started, but the whole house was gone in a matter of hours. It turns out Harriett wasn't home because she had gone out to meet Hank, but no one knew that at the time. She came home and saw the house in flames and ran clear away. We all thought she was in the house too. I didn't hear a word of her for near ten years, then a neighbor of ours thought he saw her on a trip to New York, and I did some investigating and tracked her down. It took her over a year to respond to my telegram, but she eventually did and even came down here once, in 1961, to see the graves. Whole family is out in Lincoln Memorial Park. Hank Kelly did finally marry, to a girl from Cuba, but they both died of the flu in '54.

Enemy

I can feel the ghost inside me
beating. She rolls over while I
lie still, she dances all the time.
The incessant tap tap tap tap tap tap
tapping of her feet plays out my body in
twitching fingers, only steady
when—

I used to listen to her but she got lost
inside me and we can't commune.
She doesn't understand why I am crying all the time.
She falls so easily to temptation, she wants to shake
me off and she wants to eat everything and she
misses touching other bodies and she longs to rush out
into crowds, smiling—I am trying to shut her off.

Pushing her out of my body, she's persuading it
to live and we should die. Think of my brothers'
burning hands. She is all on fire and I feel it, I walk
around people and try not to touch animals or dry paper,
my fingers leave scorch marks. I walk around with
that damned fire burning in my legs and up my sides
across my belly and over my shoulders, my heart
is always pounding, my lungs always full of smoke.
I will write her out and go I will write her out and leave I

will write her out and be done and gone and fall slowly, like a
leaf.

Across Miles *(for Hank)*

Scars below your eyes, beautiful boy, are you making me true?
Washing me down to what my base bones are, gentle and
panicked?
But I've got the calming hands,
the touch of your scent. Delicious you,
in any formation, hands and head in my lap, darling, gorgeous,
glorious, and the ease of the knowing. It is you, and it is me:
check.

Even my nightmares of you are beautiful. You pour me
down to what I am hiding, you remind me of the under impulse.
I say: I am not that girl anymore, and you show me a mirror.
Oh forgetfulness. The feel of your skin alights in my hands
like the fire—I try to wave away your softness. Your obvious
belonging to me. This will only bust me open in the end. You're
only as true as I can paint you.

And where are your hands! When I am digging through burning
rubbish, searching, desiring, where is your help? Your promise
to be beside me? The ten minutes I spent alone, my body frozen
as my entire life smoked away— your hands quickly melted in
the flames. The thought of you, evaporated. I left as if you were
already a corpse, my apologies! My love was a liquid thing.

For Constantine

Let's go to the creek, Harriett,
perhaps we can catch something—

and you did, always, caught
everything in any air around you.

You soaked up dictionaries and
field guides and gossip and your world grew,

and so you passed to me. You passed
to me.

> Boy boy boy
> I was barely a girl
> and they told me
> *brother.*

I couldn't know
the difference.

You learned words I couldn't understand:
I, me, you, mine, yours,

apart

Later you disappeared from my life
for days at a time,
I saw you, I could touch you
but you looked at me with
stranger eyes. With your eyes,
which were not like mine.

Childhood

One day a mountain grew
over the breakfast table.

Right out of our bowls of
grits, we watched

rocks and cliffs ascend
sliding swiftly up towards

the fresh-painted ceiling.
Never you mind that,

just think how you'll grow,
if you finish your bowls. We all

wanted to be bigger. We all wanted
to grab the globe by our palms and

drag our enormous fingers
across it.

For Constantine

You a mirror
of my face.
The mirror
melting away—
waving glass.

Your deeper eyes,
thicker lashes.
You say (in my dreams)
only a tickle, it's—

But did you laugh,
did you kick
the flames as though
their fingers were mine

Relentlessly tickling you?

Ms. Evelyn "Evie" Wright, roommate and longtime friend
Interviewed by John Friedman in August 1969

Oh, Harriett. That girl could really keep a ghost.

Do you know, I remember the very first time I saw her? She never knew this, but I watched her for almost an hour before I approached her. It was in Virginia—1946 –I'm sure it was September. I had been down to visit an aunt of mine that lived outside of Richmond, and was heading back to town to catch a morning train to New York. She was standing by a road sign, eyes glazed and half –closed... just standing there. It looked like she was hitching, but when cars passed, she didn't even blink. She was clutching a small paper bag in her left hand; I can see her now, just like a photograph. Holding that arm close to her body while the other jutted out, almost as if it were broken, like it was running away from her body. Her dress, too, was hanging away from her like it couldn't bear to touch her skin. God, I loved her in an instant. I mean, how can you see something so lonesome and not have your heart cling to it?

Of course, I didn't have any sisters of my own. I was the first girl born in my family since my great-grandmother. But I knew right away I wouldn't ever leave her alone. She was mine, you see? I simply couldn't.

So I took her with me. She moved into my room and at first I did everything for her. She barely moved from her bed. Imagine my surprise to come home one day to a full southern feast, like she'd been at it all day. She wasn't too fair a cook, everything was overcooked or burnt, but from then on she did whatever she could to make her own way a little. She joined the brothel, which I never encouraged, but I guess it did her some good to get out every now and again. And that's how she met Theo— though, try as I did to keep them together and all, he turns around and pulls her away from me, like he could really take care of her! Well, he ended up bringing her right back. Harriett knew I was the only one who knew her. We were two parts of one piece.

I'm sure you've heard the stories about the nightmares, and the poems, and it's all true. She woke me up screaming one morning, and I rushed over to her bed to find her face and hands covered in ink—I thought she'd slept with a pen in her hand. She was still weak, and so upset, that I carried her myself down the hall to the bath. When I went to gather the dirty sheets for the wash, I noticed there weren't just smudges, there were words. And these were the most terrifying, gruesome poems about burning flesh!

Uneasy

I don't dream
of tragedies.

My nightmares
consist
of things like
flowers
blooming softly,

a midday nap
alone in a field.
Peace

leaves me uneasy—

Evie's Advice

Evie says I should
just let my new life surround me, like

freshly ironed shirts
or the morning
can make up for anything.

Off the Rails

I am sitting on the train, squeezed between two elderly women surrounded by shopping sacks.

I am thinking about a river I see in my dreams, how it churns up into a wave and crashes over my house, a thousand miles and 13 years away, extinguishing everything. I don't mind the choke.

> "I was in love
> with a woman
> once."

A voice rings out loud and rich across the train. I glance down the car and see a man in a dark brown suit, his back turned to the car, his forehead pressed against the window. He repeats:

> "I was in love
> with a woman
> once."

I mark the unnatural curve of his shoulders, his back still held straight, his legs braced in identical angles. He holds his fingertips as if he's playing a piano.

> "But I didn't know
> how to express
> my love."

No, I think, *we never know*. I observe a slight twitch in his right knee, as if about to bow under this incredible weight. I don't notice that I have dropped my purse.

> "I took
> my friend's love letters,
> I put
> my name on them."

I imagine my arms slowly reaching around his waist, raising my hands to press palm-down over his heart. I imagine one slow, deep breath, mine released a whistle, his, a heavy sigh. I imagine pressing my left cheek against his left shoulder, pulling his body back into mine. I rock slowly forward against him, breathing that low, hollow whistle.

> "I couldn't kiss her
> without feeling
> dishonest."

I feel the gear in my stomach turn and burst. My eyes begin to water and I blink. I see him clearly. I am counting the footsteps between us, but I do not move. I watch his hands curl into fists, and press against the door, pushing his body away from it. His face rises. I sit straighter. He shoves his hands into his pockets and turns, just as the train pulls into the station. It stops and he walks boldly off, not even a glace in my direction. I release a breath I didn't realize I was holding. The old ladies stare past me at the door he has just walked through. I breathe, collect my purse from the floor. Think about shards of glass.

Hank.

Hank

> I have never wanted
> anything like you

You put up a wall
for me to climb
over, you said:

Scale gracefully.
I bit your challenge.

> I have never wanted
> anyone like
> I want you

I don't know
how to move
these thoughts

away from your hands.

Such gorgeous
consequence, when
you took mine and pulled
me apart from the rest
and said:

you, Harriett,
specifically.
When I am alone,

I remember this,
and say yes.

Coffee

I sat down
at the counter and
ordered a small coffee
and biscuit, honey
on the side. The waitress
made a slight nod
to her left. I glanced
down the counter and I
saw him.

Constantine, taller and
broader, crossed the diner
until he stood, a grown man
by my side. He put
his hand on my shoulder,
I buried my face in his shirt
pockets.

He said he missed
the way I laughed.
He said the fire
felt like feathers.

To Theo Block

I haven't admitted
anything, you know,
not to anyone
thicker than my shadow.

Good luck
stringing me up by this,
I haven't even
woven the rope,
you got
a noose made of
clouds, my friend.

But come and
get me, I'm not afraid.
I'll hold my hands
in my pockets, I'll
stretch out
my neck. Or would you
rather I fell
to the bed
in a frenzy?
Of what?
Love for you?

You have no idea
who I know you are.

How I Fell

Theo sat
at the very edge
of the plush
purple velvet sofa.
I was crouched before him,
pulling apart my bed
sheets searching for the one
poem I wanted. While I
tangled, I absent-mindedly
recited a short bit of Keats
I had first read
a few days before.

It had soaked right in.
This living hand, I whispered,
now warm and capable
of earnest grasping—

He says something in his heart
startled and before he realized,
he had grabbed my hand. I wasn't
surprised, but looked plainly
at his emboldened extension.
I noticed a long, thick scar
breaking directly across his knuckle.

Just like Hank—

and I glanced up
into familiar brown eyes.

This is how I fell.

Miss Molly Eunice Peters, fellow whore in the brothel
Interviewed by John Friedman in December 1977

We had no idea where she came from. Just showed up one day and stayed 'round. Nobody minded, and she never said much, at first. Later as she adjusted to things, we got real close.

I don't know about anyone else but she told me she knew I was special. Made for somethin' more. She was the quiet kind to push ya, like, would climb up a tree to show you that you could do it too.

Oooh and then Mr. Block! Lord! He took a liking to her straightaway and she would have none of it! I would've followed that man to the North Pole, and here was Harriett, talking about some boy she knew as a girl. Yes, Hank Kelly, can you believe she was still sweet on him after all that time?! But Block was serious, and he kept after her. One day she comes up to me, all pale and wide-eyed and like she's seen a ghost. I ask her what's up and she rambles on about Hank dead and coming for her. She was hysterical. So we put her in a room and told her to get some rest. Block comes and we send him up, thinking a fight with him would knock the silly right outta her. Instead they come down together an hour later, both beaming like newlyweds, and walk straight out the house. Not a word to anyone! We heard nothing for a few weeks, then Harriett came right back to work, like normal. But she confessed just to me later, that she was in love with Hank and Theo brought him back and all sorts of crazy talk. I pushed for details about Block, and she only said that she loved him but he was trying to get her to quit the brothel. She seemed determined to stay though, and he, no matter what change had come over her, still knew better than to challenge her.

I will say—and though I did love Harriett, so dearly—but I will admit I was always jealous of her. Block started publishing her books of poems and her life really took a good turn, for a bit. At one point, she took a trip down to Florida to meet with some old family friend. She hadn't been back at all since that fire that killed her family. And she never talked about it. But she came back a little off, then quit the brothel and shut herself up from everybody, even me... she disappeared. And when Block tried to break in to her new apartment, they had some huge fight that landed him in jail for the night and Harriett in the hospital, for nerves. When she got out she wouldn't let Evie look after her (not that I blame her for that!) and I stepped in. In a week or so she was well on her way back, even tried patching things up with Evie and Block. But I don't believe that she was ever the same again, you could see it in her face. She moved in with Block but kept a room with Evie as well. I began to hear from her less and less. And then I moved out here to Chicago and I haven't been back. I do still care for her though. Don't let anyone doubt that.

Love

to Hank:

The first time I moved slowly—
underwater.
As if my whole life,
I had been standing in mud,
clayed in, and I was being
waterfalled free. Things
around me slowed
and stopped. Even you
were frozen. Only I moved

towards you
as though my life...

Out of breath arrived
By your side: You my

lifeboat,
rope,
oxygen tank.

And now so sudden
You return under
                   his face
Nothing slows, nothing swells
The world bursting around us
and you
             bursting around me

Meditation on Guilt

Today is not
the day
it should've grown up to be,

hitting noontime
with empty hands

Honey you've got
miles to go,
mountains to fell. Better
get moving

better get alive

Today

I tried to wash
my dirty sheets

I know this
should be
an easy task, but
I have troubles:
I can always
find the pen, but not
always paper, I always
wake

with a poem on my lips

and no tape. *Better*
write that down, better
get it out
out out, better—

(My punishment stands:
boils, and flesh eaten

from the inside!)—

Spots growing
on my hands
like the pox.

Maybe I'm just
sensitive to the ink.
maybe I'm dreaming

The children only cry
for ointment, they never
blame me

I don't think
they know it's my fault.

For Constantine

Bringer of poetry and light
words into my dark world—you,

Taught me unhappiness. Showed me
the consequence of a single blade

Of grass breaking. But showed me
the whistle. Things I knew, I wanted

Only to show you. How this and
for that. The great care I took to earn

The bond given me by our birth—
brother, can we two stay and wrap up

Inside our mother's burning arms,
alone recreate the womb we shared?

Can we reorder the universe? And I will
burn, while you grow on as we both deserve.

My Fears

Not that

I could lose
you, I could,

I have

I do it everyday,
about,

Not the impulse
to last—

the stay,
stay, wait,

wait—

It's the mornings
when I get
up, refurbished
and with clean hands

shining—

That I could
come

clean

Golden Beach

When I was 14, we went
to the beach. Just my father, Constantine,
and I. I fell in love with the waves and rushed out,
again and again, to feel them smash against me,
fighting my eagerness. This is before I knew
that love was not a struggle.

They beat me all day and I finally fell
underneath them just before the sun disappeared
into the horizon. The water rushed
over me, and into my nose and mouth and ears as I
blinked, looking at the surface just above me.

The sun was glinting golden on the greenish blue screen
and I dazedly reached my fingers out to trace
the motion. I thought if I felt too far, and my hand touched air,
I would never breathe again. I felt beautiful and alive
under my ocean lover, rocking me so softly now.

Constantine counted and knew I had gone too far. My father
jumped up from the sand and swam savagely to me
(he didn't know how to swim), and hauled my body
back to shore. Pressed my stomach until water forced its way
past my lips a second time, and I, choking, finally realized
what I had almost done. What had almost happened to me.

We never told my mother. Constantine and I would imagine
that drowning is just what love is like; a slow float,
your body being filled almost unnoticeably by something else,
taking your breath and eventually your heartbeat, beating
for you from the outside; the almost heaviness, the intoxicating
lightness, and the final defeat, when you are washed ashore,
beaten and bloated, and with a smile on your face.

Escape

Those first days come back to me
in quiet moments,
sometimes
waiting for a bus
on an empty street,
or staring into closed shop windows.
More than anywhere,
I remember in the shower.
Rain still pelts like acid,
fire-water, guilt and
regret wash over me—

I walked up the path, towards
my own backyard. Hank had
turned back, had to hurry
home as well. I held my hands
out to feel every branch, every
leaf and flower all soft kisses
on my skin. My blood was
bursting through my veins,
and I felt my mouth grinning
when I heard the rustling—

It was windy and I smelled
smoke. Panicked. Knew the
truth in the pit of my stomach.
Seconds later I burst through
the last bush and saw my
home aflame, the orange
monster fluttering and
cackling. There was nothing to
do. The top floor had already
collapsed. Not a soul to feel. I
turned and walked back to the
road, too distracted to follow

the path this time. I walked for
as long as I could, and fell, and
suffered nightmares alone in a
swampy yard.

Eventually hunger came back to me.
Sooner than I would've liked,
but I was too appreciative
of the scents wafting from Mrs. Daily's kitchen.
My mouth watered
for the first two days
while I tried to resist.
Finally my body forced me to give in
and I ate—a bowl of turkey stew.
I couldn't keep it down though,
and was sick all night.

Mr. & Mrs. Paul and Millicent Daily, hosts in Davie, FL
Interviewed by John Friedman in 1978

"It was the strangest thing: I come up over that hill, just over yonder, and see this lump, this thing. I come up close on it; I had my rifle in my hand, ready for anything. Wasn't expecting any type of girl, no sir! And she was so dirty, it was hard to tell that was even what she was. Just a muddy, scratched up thing. I judged she was still breathing, hard and raspy, and carried her myself back over the mile to my place. My wife, she saw me coming and looked as if I was crazy, couldn't tell what it was either. She screamed, later told me she thought I had accidented and shot one of the neighbors' boys; they use to cause a load of trouble out in the swamps, that's true. But we put her right down on the porch, and my wife brought out rags and water and cleaned her up right there. I went in for breakfast. Millie, that's my wife, she can be real fussy if you try to help her out. But I remember, I had a nice hot plate of ham and eggs, my favorite..."

"Oh, she came to us in quite a state! A veritable wreck, I'll tell you. But I washed her up and had Paul carry her into the guest room. She slept in fits for three days. When she woke, wouldn't eat or speak. It reminded me of a time when I was a little girl, and my brothers brought home a wounded rabbit. They gave it to me to doctor up, and though I had a feeling they were the cause of the poor thing's wounds, I took great care trying to nurse her back to health. She did heal, but was never quite right. Wouldn't eat if you were watching, and shuddered something fearful anytime anyone other than me held her. Eventually she died of fright—one of my cousins tried to feed her and she just fell over dead. I was heartbroken. But my brothers were feeling merciful and helped me give her a proper funeral. I get teary just thinking of it. That poor rabbit. But yes, Harriett was on edge the entire time she was with us."

Dark Body

There was a dark body,
loosely wrapped in dirty cloth,
twisted up as if it had drowned against the ceiling
in the easternmost corner of my room.
Its wet hair hung limply and swayed if I
rushed through the room.

It changed size, some days
as small as a grasshopper, others so large
that it filled the entire room, and I could not enter
without touching it, or breathe
without getting dirt
in my mouth.

It stayed with me for years.
I came to need it close to me.

One morning, without ceremony, I awoke and
it was gone.
I walked to the window
and lifted the shade
and let the light in.

To Theo (after the fight)

How you came quietly.
How I came along,
unwittingly tripped
onto the knife. Yes,
I cried. But I cry
all the time. You will
forgive me? How I am
not brave, how I am
all consequence, all
cocked triggers.
I don't expect you to
be gentle. Don't expect
me to be kind.

After

This morning
the line took ten minutes to come.
I could feel it,
like a fishbone caught
in my throat, like the cough
I held after inhaling
my first cigarette. It itched
its way so slowly out.

It was the slowest poem.

And it was filled with light from the sun
not the fire and it breathed breezes not
smoke. It twinkled like a joke. And I laughed!

This morning I woke up,
and I laughed.

For Constantine

Confederate soul I fought with needles.
You sunk heavy into sands I couldn't swallow.
You gnawed through every rope.
Even the ligaments of heart-flesh.
That was mine, was yours.

Everytime you turn around.
My back bears flames, churning.
Our ending already written in dust.
Even the water on fire, I could not stop.
Your cries at any offering I hold.
Bear through, burn through.

To the morning when you reappear.
I forgiven, wind pushed through the door.
On fire, hand in hand pull you living.
Back beside my own brick face.
Tearing it down I awake.

It was a heavy walk through the Floridian swamps. Fire under her fingernails, fever in her heart. She developed the slow blink. Gasping breath. Irregular spasms of joy. Absorbed in guilt, she croons of lost hearts and the spaces we left abandoned. **HARRIETT VAN OS**, of fire-breathers, tamed the hunger. What results is waste. Her poems, this story, seeping from her bones like sweat onto these sheets.

LAUREN HUNTER is from North Carolina and lives in Brooklyn. She received her MFA in poetry from The New School and reads as Harriett Van Os with The Poetry Brothel. She has recently joined the team at Telephone Books as their Emperor of Ice Cream. Her poems can be found online in *pax americana, Lyre Lyre,* and *Food I Corp Publishing Enterprise.* She hates to sleep and loves to dance.

BROTHEL BOOKS, The Poetry Society of New York's newest imprint, is a small book publisher based in New York City. The Poetry Brothel has long been a proponent of bringing poetry to the masses--exclusively, and with absolute discretion. Likewise, The Poetry Brothel's publishing arm, Brothel Books, publishes the most intimate, most charming, and most crafted works being produced today, primarily by The Poetry Brothel's poets across the globe, but also the general public.